Coming to America

Marcus McArthur, Ph.D.

Consultants

Shelley Scudder
Gifted Education Teacher
Broward County Schools

Caryn Williams, M.S.Ed.
Madison County Schools
Huntsville, AL

Publishing Credits

Conni Medina, M.A.Ed., *Managing Editor*
Lee Aucoin, *Creative Director*
Torrey Maloof, *Editor*
Marissa Rodriguez, *Designer*
Stephanie Reid, *Photo Editor*
Rachelle Cracchiolo, M.S.Ed., *Publisher*

Image Credits: Cover, pp. 1, 8, 18, 26
Alamy; p. 21 Associated Press; p.9 Getty
Images; pp. 17, 23, 27–29 iStockphoto; p. 29
Jayden Acosta; pp. 25 (left & right), 32 Kim
Delevett; pp. 14–15, 15, 22(left) National
Archives; pp. 20, 24 Newscom; p. 19 The
Granger Collection; p. 2–3 The Library of
Congress [LC-USZC2-1255]; p.5 The Library
of Congress [LC-DIG-ggbain-03252]; p. 6
The Library of Congress [LC-USZ62-7307];
p. 7 The Library of Congress
[LC-DIG-ppmsca-17886]; p.10 The Library
of Congress [LC-USZ62-20877]; p. 11 The
Library of Congress [LC-USZC4-5545]; p. 12
The Library of Congress [LC-USZ62-7386];
p. 13 The Library of Congress
[LC-DIG-highsm-17027]; p. 16 The Library
of Congress [LC-DIG-ggbain-02970];
p. 22(right) The Library of Congress
[LC-USZC4-4940]; All other images from
Shuttestock.

Teacher Created Materials
5301 Oceanus Drive
Huntington Beach, CA 92649-1030
http://www.tcmpub.com
ISBN 978-1-4333-6997-1
© 2014 Teacher Created Materials, Inc.

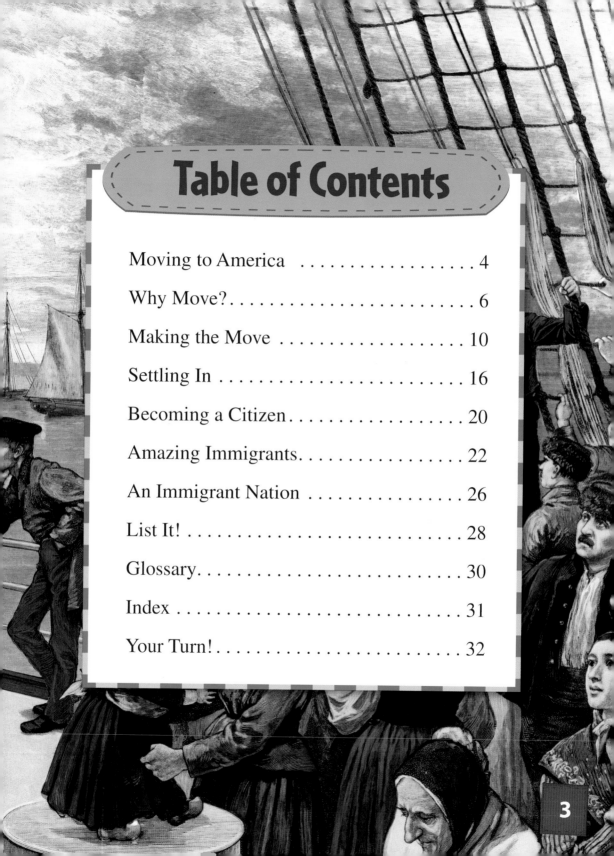

Table of Contents

This family is moving to a new country.

Moving to America

Has your family ever moved to a new place? You may have moved to a new city or state. Leaving home can be hard. It means going to a new school. It means making new friends.

These immigrants are arriving in America in the early 1900s.

Imagine moving to a new country. People who leave their homes to live in a new country are called **immigrants** (IM-i-gruhntz). There are many immigrants in America. They have come from different countries around the world.

Why Move?

Immigrants leave their home countries for many reasons. Some move to America to get away from war. They want to live in a place where they are safe. Other immigrants want to get away from bad leaders. They come to America to be treated fairly.

These immigrants are on their way to America in 1902.

There are also immigrants who leave their home countries because of their **beliefs**. They may get treated badly for what they believe. Or they may not get to practice their **religion**. They come to America so they can have the freedom to believe what they want.

These kids came to America from China.

Some immigrants leave because their home countries are too crowded. There are not enough jobs and homes for all the people who live there. So they come to America to find places to live and work.

This family came to America from Mexico.

Many immigrants come to America looking for new **opportunities** (op-er-TOO-ni-teez). Opportunities are chances to do things and succeed (suhk-SEED). Immigrants may want a better life. Many immigrants think dreams can come true in America. All it takes is hard work. This idea is called the *American Dream*.

This advertisement from 1919 tells immigrants what America can offer them.

Making the Move

Long ago, it was not easy to travel to America. Many immigrants came by ship. They had to sell everything they had to buy a ticket. Often, they had to leave other family members and friends behind.

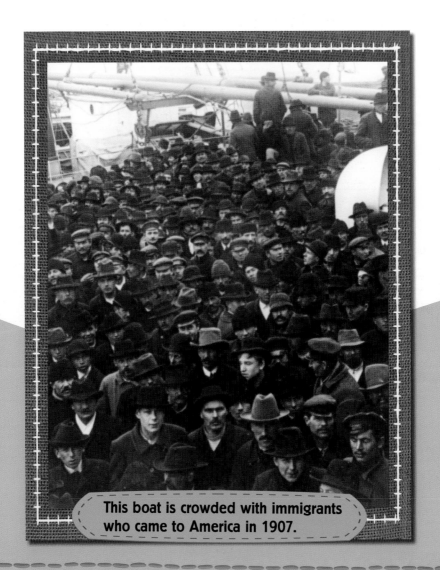

This boat is crowded with immigrants who came to America in 1907.

The trip was not easy. It could take one to two weeks. Most immigrants traveled in steerage. This was where the people stayed who paid the lowest price for their tickets. It was very dirty and crowded. People often got sick. When the immigrants arrived in America, they could not wait to get off the ship.

Third Class

Most ships were divided into three parts. The people who had lots of money traveled in first class or second class. They had their own rooms. People who did not have much money bought third-class tickets. They traveled in steerage.

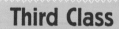

These people are on a ship headed to America in 1899.

Long ago, ships that came from Europe (YOOR-uhp) went to Ellis Island. It was an **immigration** station in New York City. On their way to the station, the ships passed the Statue of Liberty. Some immigrants saw the statue and cheered. They were happy to be in America.

Officers inspect immigrants at Ellis Island in 1913.

At the station, each immigrant had to pass a medical exam. This means that their bodies were looked at closely. They had to be healthy before they could enter America. Immigrants who were sick had to stay at the station. Sometimes, they were sent back home.

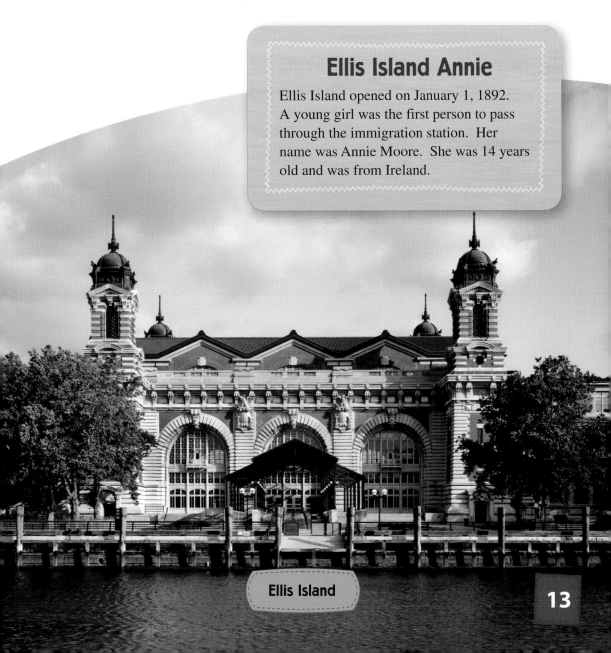

Ellis Island Annie

Ellis Island opened on January 1, 1892. A young girl was the first person to pass through the immigration station. Her name was Annie Moore. She was 14 years old and was from Ireland.

Ellis Island

Long ago, ships that came from Asia (EY-shuh) went to Angel Island. This was an immigration station, too. Most of the immigrants at this station were Chinese.

Take a Tour

Angel Island is in San Francisco, California. Today, it is a museum. You can take a tour. You can learn more about the immigrants who were held there.

Angel Island

Immigrants were not treated well at Angel Island. They were sometimes kept there for weeks. They had to stay in small, dirty cells. The cells looked like zoo cages. The immigrants were given little food. They had to have medical exams, too. They also had to answer questions about themselves. If they gave the wrong answers, they could be sent back home.

These are Chinese immigrants at Angel Island in 1923.

This is Little Italy in New York long ago.

Settling In

Being an immigrant is not always easy. Some immigrants may wear different clothes. They may eat different foods. Sometimes, immigrants do not know how to speak English.

Chinatown

There are a few Chinatowns in the United States. This one is in San Francisco, California. It is home to the largest Chinese community outside of Asia.

This is Chinatown in San Francisco today.

Long ago, immigrants were not treated well. People would hurt them for the way they looked or spoke. Immigrants wanted to feel safe. So they started **communities** (kuh-MYOO-ni-teez) of their own. A community is a group of people with the same interests who live in the same area. This is how places like Little Italy and Chinatown formed.

Some immigrants still face **prejudice** (PREJ-uh-dis). Prejudice is treating people unfairly because they are part of a certain group. Some people do not like those who are different from them. They think everyone should look the same. They think everyone should act the same. They feel uneasy when people do not.

This song from long ago tells how a girl cannot get a job because she is Irish.

These people may also feel afraid. Or they may get angry. Sometimes they are not nice. They forget that immigrants are people just like them.

This cartoon shows how America set quotas on immigration.

This immigrant is now an American citizen.

Becoming a Citizen

Some immigrants choose to become American **citizens** (SIT-uh-zuhns). Citizens are members of a country. They have rights. In America, citizens can vote for, or choose, their leaders. They can speak freely. They can have their own beliefs.

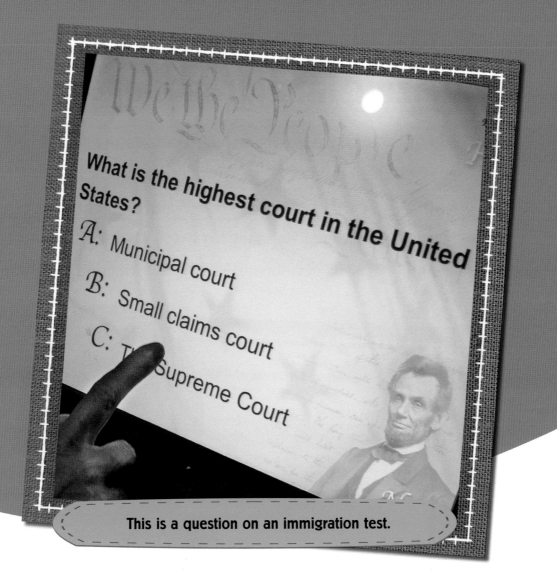

What is the highest court in the United States?

A: Municipal court

B: Small claims court

C: The Supreme Court

This is a question on an immigration test.

To become a citizen, immigrants need to live in America for five years. Then, they can take a test. They need to know American history. They also need to know about the government (GUHV-ern-muhnt). And they need to know how to speak English. If they pass the test, they become citizens!

Amazing Immigrants

Many amazing Americans have been immigrants. Some of the best thinkers came from other countries. Albert Einstein (AHYN-stahyn) was a smart scientist. He was born in Germany. He came up with new ideas about space and time. He became an American citizen in 1940.

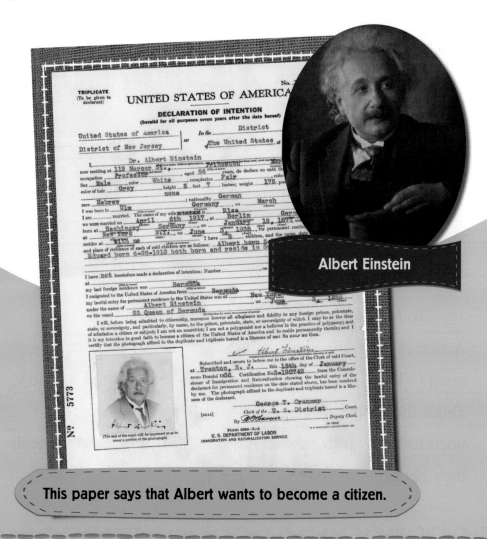

Albert Einstein

This paper says that Albert wants to become a citizen.

Have you ever worn Levi (LEE-vahy) jeans? Did you know that an immigrant designed them? Levi Strauss (STROUS) was from Europe. He came to America in 1843. He was the first to make jeans. He made them for gold miners.

This is a tag on Levi jeans.

Do you like sports? Many sports stars are immigrants. Albert Pujols is a famous baseball player. He is from the Dominican Republic. He came to America in 1996. He helped his team win the World Series in 2006.

Albert Pujols

Many immigrants have helped make America better. Not all of them are famous. Kim Delevett (DEL-uh-vet) was born in Vietnam (vee-et-NAHM). She came to America in 1975. Today, she helps other immigrants feel proud of who they are and where they came from. She gives speeches about why it is important to remember your home country and **traditions** (truh-DISH-uhnz).

This is Kim with her brother in Vietnam in 2005.

This is Kim (front) as a child with her family in Vietnam in 1975.

An Immigrant Nation

Immigrants have given America many things. They have shared their traditions and beliefs. They have also shared their ideas and skills.

This boy is celebrating with an immigrant tradition.

Immigrants also bring **diversity** (dih-VUR-si-tee) to America. Diversity means having many different kinds of people. Diversity makes our country stronger. It helps us see the world differently. We can taste foods from around the world. We can learn new ideas. In so many ways, immigrants have made America what it is today.

This group of students shows diversity.

List It!

Imagine that your family is moving to another country. List two things you will miss the most about your home. List two things that excite you about your new country.

This family is moving to a new country.

My family is moving to France.
The two things I will miss about my home are:
1. my friends
2. my school

The two things I am exited about are:
1. seeing the Eiffel Tower
2. learning to speack French

This is the boy's list.

Glossary

beliefs—thoughts and feelings that a person accepts as true or right

citizens—members of a country or place

communities—places where groups of people live and work together

diversity—having different kinds of people in a group

immigrants—people who move to another country to live there

immigration—when people move to another country to live there

opportunities—chances to do things and be successful

prejudice—treating people unfairly because they are part of a certain group

religion—a system of beliefs and rules

traditions—ways of thinking or doing things that have been used by a group of people or a family for a long time

Index

Your Turn!

Amazing Immigrants

Kim Delevett is an amazing immigrant. She helps other immigrants be proud of who they are.

Do you know an amazing immigrant? Draw a picture of the person. Then write a sentence that tells about him or her.